Surprised by Light

Surprised by Light

Ulrich Schaffer

with photographs by the author

HARPER & ROW, PUBLISHERS, San Francisco
Cambridge, Hagerstown, Philadelphia, New York
London, Mexico City, São Paulo, Sydney

1817

FIRST EDITION

Library of Congress Cataloging in Publication Data

Schaffer, Ulrich
    Surprised by light.

    I. Title.
PR9199.3.S26S9   1980   811'.54   80–7751
ISBN 0–06–067086–X

80 81 82 83 84 10 9 8 7 6 5 4 3 2 1

for all those
who still delight in the beauty of the world,
who are fascinated
by the interconnectedness of all

for all those
who still want to see and feel
and want to risk vulnerability
by being sensitive

Again and again the miracle takes place:
the amazing transformation
in which the air turns into leaves
and the earth becomes roots,
in which the sun fills the seed to the bursting,
then lets it break open and sprout.
New life breaks through
in the transformation of death.

We are sustained by the surprise of the miracle,
by the change of the seasons,
and I am a link in this miraculous chain.
In me the unchangeable
also changes
and I know
that I would break
the rhythm of creation
if I did not change.
I would be dead to life,
even if I continued to live.

I am not yearning for great miracles,
but for the daily change,
the almost imperceptible rebirth,
the insignificant miracle of growth,
which is greater than all others.

When our eyes will be opened
for that which has been,
we will see that he was always with us:
beside us at birth
    midwife and doctor
when taking the first steps
    father and mother
in the shock of death and catastrophe
    counselor and comforter
in disappointed love
    as friend and lover
in the overwhelming demand of life
    as one still having hope in us
in the despair of having no way out
    as the old but always new way
in death
    as a strong hand with promise of life
and we will see
    that when he was absent
    he was close to us.

Here,
flat on the ground,
pressed into the grass,
I don't expect anything or anyone.
Here
I experience the world
of bugs and plants,
without history
or any relationship to the momentous events
of the world.
Here
I can hide
better than anywhere else,
and I can believe that everything is fine.

But then the earth moves
and in the gentle wind
which bends and holds the grasses
God meets me.

Once again
where I have not expected him.

He surrounds us with astonishing gentleness,
comes close to us in silence.
He is in the waving grass,
in the yellow, blue and red
and their million hues.

He sinks deep into our soul
and raises a joy
that is almost imperceptible, yet strong.
He plows the furrow
into which he throws the seed
which swells and sprouts
and grows toward him.

He expands like a sound,
like a joyous laugh,
like a word
from which the world comes into being.

He is a miracle of closeness
in tenderness yet strength.
He is here!

I need time,
uncluttered time,
to center myself,
to gather myself in.

I want to find the center again
that will keep my life together.
I want to look into my own eyes,
to become quiet
in order to be able to love again.

God offers himself as center,
as axis around which all revolves,
as the core of all things.

He is the circle in which we are free,
and in the circle the cross
onto which we fall
and from which we rise again
to a life of love.

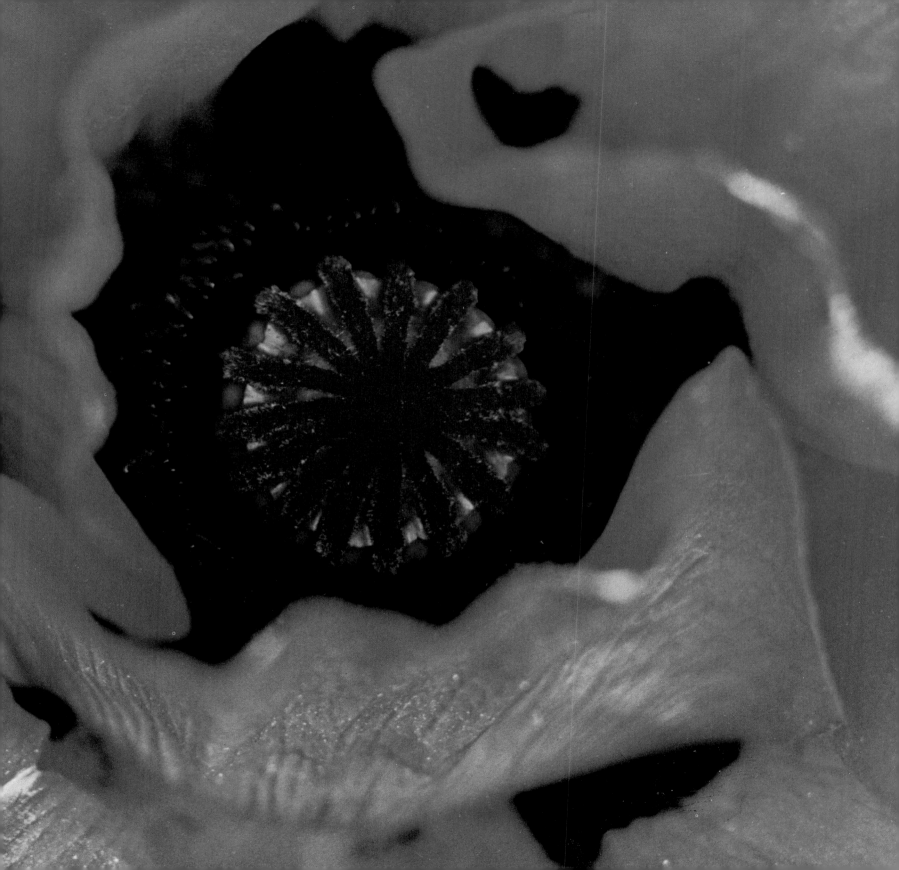

I notice
that I am vulnerable
to death
and that sheds light on me.

The ground disappears from under my feet
when I feel strong.
I become weak, yet strong,
when I have nothing to lose.

I sacrifice my senses
but regain them,
transformed by going under
in fear and need.

Fear saves me from contentment,
in which I fall asleep and die.
Need creates in me the search for more,
which makes me rich.

In opening myself to hurt
tears become solid rocks,
and from the wounds we share
strength flows to all.

Relying on the power of his stroke
the swimmer will sink;
while struggling to survive
the sinking one will learn to swim.

He creates the yearning in you
    that at times seems too much to bear.
He allows you to think paradise
    even though you cannot enter it yet.
He lets you become restless
    so that you will start wandering again
    through the thousand thoughts of the world.
He shows you the incompleteness of everything
    because only one image and one presence
    will still your yearning.

He gives out waiting and yearning
    like a gift and a heaviness,
because he alone
    can satisfy our hunger.

It seems as if he would choose not to live here,
but move on in search of a place
where he could be radiant.

But then suddenly he appears.
He overwhelms me,
tears open my heart,
pours himself into it
and leaves me speechless.

With so much closeness
I have to flee behind closed eyelids,
like Moses long ago.

We ask ourselves what is behind it all
and meet the unanswerable a thousand times
and yet continue to be drawn
to the many doors of life.

We hesitate, but want to go on.
We are fearful, but want to learn.
We are timid, but want to be courageous.
We shrink back, and yet want to grow.

We have to take courage and jump.
We have to cut the ropes and set ourselves adrift.
We have to leave the solid ground to learn to swim.
We have to sacrifice our security and take risks.

Then we will experience God as the hand in the abyss,
as the net under the high wire,
as lifeboat on the high seas,
as ground under our feet.

To be
is miracle enough.
To sense that I am,
here,
in this time,
in this space,
so unique and special.
One day I appeared on this earth
and said: I am I.
That is miracle enough.

In the endless, empty spaces of the universe,
in the mystery of the secret workings
of all things,
it is the greater wonder
that I am,
that I fill the emptiness
with life,
that I experience myself
and know about myself,
and that I then penetrate to the outside
and meet you.

I will not search for miracles
but become conscious
that I am miracle enough.
I will celebrate myself
as God celebrates me.

This world swallows the sound of my feet,
allows me the silence of meditation,
receives me into itself,
makes me tender and sensitive.

I
stand
still
and sense growth all around me.

Guided by a hidden hand
the secret connections of the world
reveal themselves to me
and I sense the breathing order of all life.

And in the meadow under the trees
and the flower on the meadow
and the caterpillar on the flower
and in the light on the bark of the tree
and the bark hugging the trunk of the tree
and the trunk reaching into the indescribable blue
he becomes visible,
who receives me into himself,
and makes me silent.

The circle of love is completed
in me.

Senses open the world to us.
Life flows in through the eyes.
Ears pick up sound
and the skin feels the lightest touch.
The tongue tastes the smallest gradations
and the nose opens yet another world.

The world streams in
and overwhelms us.

But then the senses are too narrow,
their framework bursts,
a stronger yearning for completeness is opened up,
and like a wound, yet celebration,
it moves us far beyond ourselves
into a deeper realm,

where only God can teach us
through his Holy Spirit
what we so deeply yearn for.

Where voluntary silence spreads,
there is hope for language again.

Where eyes learn to give up tantalizing images,
visions can again become possible.

Where ears can abandon harmonious sounds,
prophecies can be heard.

Where we have time again,
the timeless will be present.

Where the visible points beyond itself,
the invisible will become discernible again.

You reach deeper than any abyss
and farther than any starry nebula.
Even in the black holes of the universe
you are still the absolute law.

I cannot hide from you.
I expect you at every turn
and don't need to beg for your presence.

I inhale you.
I talk to you.
I stand in your presence.
You have exhaled me.
You answer me.
We meet.

The sense of wonder passes over and through me
like a large never-ending wave.

Nothing but a thin security
is our tent.
And our house is a life
from hand to mouth
because we cannot live from reserves
nor die from reserves.
Not even the small death.

We can lose our security
when a cloud passes before the sun
or when the sun is too bright.
Then our security splits open
like a ripe fruit in a thunderstorm
and fear shows itself as the core.
It is not fear of the end of the world,
nor fear of the bottomless abyss,
but of the slow decline,
of living without light
in the shadows of unimportance.

But because you are also the keeper of my fear,
I will meet that fear.
I want to see if my faith stops
or if grace burns through my hand
as a star of hope that is too large
to contain.

I want to see the fear split,
and you, Lord, as its core,
indivisible.

One day I will be with you.
I will stand in your presence,
tired of wandering,
weary of the inconsequential.

Then I want to bathe in innocence
and experience the freedom of the children of God.
I will lay aside my failures
like old clothing.

Then I will know what holiness is:
to be chosen
to be near you
and to survive the fire of your purity.

Until then I will look for your presence here.
And if tiredness should affect me,
I will invoke the innocence and freedom
you have granted your children.

Your kingdom is already growing in me.
I meet you as you spread out in me
and shape the landscape of my life
after your will.

I am walking towards the perfection
for which now I can only hope.

Sometimes your silence
comes upon me like a bird of prey
and I turn into a scurrying mouse
searching for shelter
in the noisy world of distractions.

Swiftly and silently you follow me,
search out my hiding place
and tear my noise away from me.
Painfully you cut out
the sound of voices,
dismiss my friends
and let my words return to me empty.

Once more you become the God of burnt offerings
requesting that I sacrifice the flight into words,
to stand in silence
before your burning bush
and to feel the holy ground searing my feet,
to get a glimpse of the silent dove descending.

What you have taken from me
you return a hundredfold,
and love grows out of sacrifice.

Without its weight
the anchor would not hold the boat.

Without resistance
the muscle would not grow.

Without tension
the bow would not shoot the arrow.

Without weight
the seed would not remain in the earth.

Without ballast
the balloon could not be steered.

Without the gravity of the world
I would fly away,
neither have nor give security
and be without understanding
for the heaviness of the world.

He meets you in gentleness.
He comes close.
He takes your coldness
and warms you from the inside.

You can melt,
and if you do,
streams will flow from you
to give life and renew the land.

Light gives the world its shape,
makes colors visible, casts shadows
and determines the passage of time.
Light allows the world to enter us through our eyes.

But too much light singes our feet,
burns our eyes and dries us up.
And so we live in the precarious balance
of not-too-much and yet-enough,

to survive in our frailty.

The world is unclear,
the future beyond us;
even the past is not sharply in focus.
Feelings cannot be expressed precisely,
thoughts cannot be thought to their end.
Little is tangible.
Only the superficial can be explained.

And yet this lack of clarity and this uncertainty
provide our lives with the tension,
with the sense of surprise,
which keep us awake and alert.

In this tension,
while struggling for clarity,
new attitudes grow in us.
While facing insecurity
we learn to trust and believe.
Feelings for which we have never found words
now find expression.

If we don't only resist the weight of the world
it will begin to serve us.

New horizons of love will become visible.

Images rise up so visibly in me
that I could paint them.
Clouds with golden edges
allow me to fly away with them
into those landscapes which live in me:

Rocky islands
     only a few feet above the water line.
A dying salmon with purple-red tigerstripes
     in water much too shallow.
After miles of unprotected openness finally poplars
      and the underside of their leaves like coins
      in the vast prairie sky.
Rafts of logs that look like matches
     in the inlets belonging to the killer whales.
Hostile woods around the chain of lakes
     in the lostness of the evening.
The liberation that comes
     with the step above the timber line.
Bridges of the north,
     collapsed under the weight of the vastness of this country.
Craggy cliffs,
     which I can feel with the fingers of my eyes.

I become transparent
like the landscape
and pervious to another light.

I know God on paper
and in my mind.
I can talk about him
and inspire others for him.
I am convinced of his love for me.
I trust him and know
that everything will be well with me.

And yet an emptiness
which frightens me
presses into my mind.
A strong yearning for a deeper meeting
awakens in me.
An expectation spreads out in me
and I hope to be gripped
because I also want to know God in my feelings.

God, I want to experience you more totally.
I want to receive you with my entire being.
I want to become helpless
in your overwhelming presence . . .

. . . and then he fulfills my wish,
takes me far beyond words,
surprises me,
sweeps me off my feet
and releases my dammed-up yearning.
He is here!
He is here!

You are here!
Your presence moves me so profoundly
that I lose my composure.
And yet I still stand opposite you.
I am still I,
the creation before the creator,
and I give my love to you
as I receive your love.

Nothing can comprehend you,
nothing can apprehend you.
You pass through me in waves.
The limitations of my body
cannot hold you.
I am confused but filled with joy.
You have taken hold of me
and healed me with your presence.

The world blooms under the hand of God
and awakens in us the joy of living,
even under the threat of clouds.

God,
here I will stand
to fulfill
what your faith in me
expects.
I will take the desert upon myself,
the absence of your answers,
your multifaceted, eloquent silence,
to allow the fruit of solitude
to ripen in me
as nourishment for others.

I will not run away,
even when I become afraid
of the endless sand,
of the senselessness,
you silent one,
because you are never far.

Behind the dune
are your footsteps,
you remain unrecognized
in the wind driving the sand.
Above all is the sky,
your understanding eye.

Even the sand receives its boundaries from you.

Sometimes I am successful
at living without a specific purpose:
I am not weighed down by wishes,
I don't manipulate others or myself,
I don't worry about the future,
I just am,
a lily in the field.

What I so desperately pursued
falls into my lap
because someone is taking care of me.

Secretly you operate behind us,
in the lowlands and the mountain ranges,
in territories still unknown to us.
You are the friendly enemy
that sheds our blood to save us.

In all things you surprise us,
are suddenly there:
camouflaged in the mousy gray of boredom,
as living flame burning our feet;
you walk on water and reach out to us.
Skinned you send us through the desert,
even without a pillar of smoke or fire.

With your knee on our chest
we give up what separates us from you.
You teach us to be light and transparent
and focused only on you.

In your bold love
you become our friend
and slowly we learn
that first is last
and death is life.

The world rotates,
turns upside down
and so is finally rightside up.

With you I can experience the world anew
because in your presence everything is transformed.
You penetrate and lead back to the origin.
Nothing remains untouched by you.

The stone turns into your stone.
The beach becomes the beach
on which you meet me.
The tree rising into the endless skyblue
becomes a symbol of your creation
and takes me with it.

I can't and won't escape you
and yet I don't feel constrained
or at your mercy
because your love is visible behind all.

Nothing seems exhausted
and every design in the world
is like a new cast from your hand.
I will follow you
until I will be allowed to touch you.
Until then I will believe in you
even without putting my fingers into your wounds.

Like a branch:
resilient in the wind
seeking the light
subjected to sun and rain
fed by the roots from the depths
transforming light into energy
constantly prepared to grow
naked and ready for the winter cold
beautiful in the wealth of its flowers
bearing fruit

to be a branch,
a branch on the vine
and a bough on the tree
planted by the fresh water.

When rain carves up the land
and solid earth melts into streams
the soil is rushed into the sea;
nothing seems safe any longer.
We are once again engulfed by an angry God.

But into this grave of water,
into this drowning life,
falls hope in breaking clouds,
and with the aid of wind
we are surprised by light.

And learn again
that hope is much more durable than death,
that in the end
the seven-colored light dries up the land
and gives us life again.

The laws of life
surround me like nets.
Painful are the limitations
in which the body, soul and spirit live
and the love I practice is inadequate.

I am caught,
I rebel
but become powerless
and ready to give up in despair.

But then the call to freedom stirs in me.
My imagination comes alive
and will not recognize
the confines of this prison.

As I push out the boundaries
I realize that fear had set my limits.
I throw caution to the wind
and now live at the edge,
where worlds collide
and insights bloom more stunningly
in the face of danger.

On good days
I receive a foretaste
of the freedom
that is my final goal.

These leaves will fall,
their gold will perish.
But they will continue to live in me
as catchers of light,
as hope for life.

They will come again,
faintly in the uncertain spring green
but then powerfully conquering winter,
messengers of the same light.

Their creator and mine
has decided for life
and nothing will undo that decision,
not the longest winter
nor the darkest background.

About This Book

Over two years ago *Searching for You*, a book of my black and white photography with meditative texts, was published. With great joy I now present my first color book. It has been a pleasure to work more intensively in the area of color during the last few years. Again and again I find it thrilling to try to capture the myriad of hues that surround us. I can become quite lost in the process, temporarily forgetting where I am, what day it is and what I should be doing next. But I very much cherish that kind of communication with the world around me.

Thus the photos of this book are, in a sense, a response to the landscape. To me a landscape talks and wishes a reply. I reply with my camera. I articulate my response by choosing a particular way of photographing it: a choice of lenses, light, and angle of view.

I do not want to equate God with nature, but relating to nature in this dialogue has given me a greater awareness of God the creator. As this book celebrates creation it also celebrates the creator. It is an invitation to see God's presence in nature. And then, through the more personal texts, I have brought the human being into God's creation, at times as part of the creation and at other times as partner to the creator himself.

Most people picking up a book like this relate first to the photographs. The dialogue begins with the photographs. In the texts I want to continue the dialogue in a more personal and focused way. They are not there to explain the photographs, nor are the photographs there to illustrate the texts. Both attempt to activate the inner dialogue, to encourage the reader and viewer to meditate, to enter into the process of continuous creation. This book is an invitation to enter silence and to step into the presence of God. For that reason I have, at times, not attempted a close correspondence between photo and text, to leave enough room for readers and viewers to reach silence in their own way. I would like each reader to enjoy these pages and then perhaps to reach a deeper insight into his or her own person.

I have chosen not to say much regarding the technical aspects of photography. When I shoot in color I usually use a slide film, because color separations for the printing of books can be better done from slides. I seldom use filters, with the exception of a polarizing filter which reduces reflected light and thus gives intense, saturated colors. That explains some of the deep blue skies in my photographs. I try to keep the technical side of my photography simple in order to have more time and inner freedom to see, because I believe that good photography is a matter of seeing.

Ulrich Schaffer
Burnaby, British Columbia, Canada
Spring 1980

Notes on Photos and Texts

6/7 Photo: Oak, Monterey, California, 1976. *Trees will probably always fascinate me. Perhaps it is their age and slow growth, their constancy in the quick changes of my life. Trees are often like friends to me; and when I photograph one, a quiet communication takes place between the tree and me.*

8/9 Photo: Fog, Carmel, California, 1979. *Fog clothes a landscape in magic because it covers up and creates mysteries. Our imagination is activated in an attempt to enter these mysteries.*

10/11 Photo: Poplar leaves in grasses, in the Cariboo region of central British Columbia, Canada, 1977. *When seeing and photographing scenes like this, I often think of I Kings 19:11–13. God is in the gentle, quiet voice.*

12/13 Photo: Waving grass in the Oregon dunes, 1979.

14/15 Photo: Poppy, Burnaby, British Columbia, 1975. *I feel drawn into the flower, towards a center. The notion of "being centered" has been quite important to me in the last few years. The center of the poppy can be seen as an arrangement of crosses.*

16/17 Photo: Sandbank, Chesterman Beach, near Long Beach, Vancouver Island, British Columbia, 1978. *I am always fascinated by the designs left by the receding tide. They change every few feet. I can go through a whole roll of film in a very short time. Usually I shoot a motif like this in black and white, but the combination of browns and blues seemed promising in color. I let the pattern run diagonally through the picture to create more dynamism.*

Text: *"Becoming vulnerable" has long been an important theme in my life. I practice it again and again. When I become vulnerable I become needy before God and man and that leads me to a deep communion with both.*

18/19 Photo: Agave plants on the west coast of the island of Rhodes, Greece, 1978.

20/21 Photo: Grasses, Cariboo, British Columbia, 1977. *This photo reminds me of some of the etchings and drawings of the German Renaissance artist Albrecht Dürer (1471-1528).*

22/23 Photo: Door to a farm house in Fischerhude near Bremen, West Germany, 1977.

24/25 Photo: Evening mood between Vancouver and Vancouver Island, British Columbia, 1977.

26/27 Photo: Plant in a dune, Oregon, 1979. **Text:** *We are often so preoccupied by our goals and purposes that we are unable to celebrate our existence, our being, in a childlike fashion. See also text pp. 62–63.*

28/29 Photo: Aspens, Bridge Lake, British Columbia, 1974. **Text:** *So much of life is discovering the interconnectedness of all things and beings. I suspect that everything is much more connected than we think. Paul writes in Colossians 1:16–17, "For in him [Jesus] all things were created in heaven and on earth, visible and invisible, whether thrones or dominions or principalities or authorities — all things were created through him and for him. He is before all things, and in him all things hold together."*

30/31 Photo: Spider web, Burnaby, British Columbia, 1978.

32/33 Photo: The banks of the Fraser River (flowing green-gray in the background), British Columbia, 1977.

34/35 Photo: Kelley Lake, Cariboo, British Columbia, 1977. *I noticed that by using a polarizing filter I lost all the reflected light on the blades of grass. And although normally I would have used that filter to get a more saturated green, I took it off for this photo.*

36/37 Photo: Plants, Point Lobos, near Carmel, California, 1979. **Text:** *We often begin with a certainty in our life, then lose it as we enter fear, but in the end we are even able to see God's working in the fear. We meet God everywhere. He is the ground under us.*

38/39 Photo: Sunrise in the bay of Lindos on the Island of Rhodes, Greece, 1978. *It was an enjoyable experience to get up at five in the morning with a few friends and to wait for this moment.* **Text:** *I don't want to postpone my life to the future, but sometimes I find it necessary to remind myself that this is not all, that I am moving towards a perfection which I will actually reach.*

40/41 Photo: Rapeseed, northeast of Bremen, Germany, 1977. *Because the landscape is flat and I needed a bit of height I climbed onto the roof of my car. The farmhands walking past seemed to not quite under-stand, but that didn't bother me. I was enthralled by the yellow of the field.*

42/43 Photo: Dunes with sun, Oregon, 1979. *Sometimes I like to photograph directly into the sun. I am never certain exactly what I will have on the final picture, and I like that suspense.*

44/45 Photo: Beech trees, east of Hannover, Germany, 1977. *It was raining when I took this picture. In rain, leafgreen can become very intense, but it also seems to make the landscape appear "heavy" or "weighty." I noticed that in this picture, which led me to the writing of the text.*

46/47 Photo: Rosehips in morning frost, Cariboo, British Columbia, 1977. **Text:** John 7:38.

48/49 Photo: Doorway, City of Rhodes on the Island of Rhodes, Greece, 1978.

50/51 Photo: The reflection of a farm house, Fischerhude, near Bremen, Germany, 1977. *When the photo is turned upside down, the house can be identified more easily.* **Text:** *In recent years I have thought much about the movements of life. We have to go with certain life movements, sense the rhythms of life that are constructive and make our life flow with those rhythms.*

52/53 Photo: Lanezi Lake, in the Bowron Lakes chain, British Columbia, 1978. *This lake can only be reached by canoe or kayak. It is part of a chain of lakes which is cherished by canoeists because it is still possible to experience the original Canadian wilderness on this trip. The trip around the chain takes approximately one week. I have completed it four times.* **Text:** *This text reflects some of the images and landscapes in which I have grown up. From my tenth to my twelfth year I lived on the prairie. From thirteen to eighteen I lived in Kitimat, British Columbia, a place situated just south of the Alaskan panhandle, still surrounded by wilderness. Growing up in nature like that strongly influenced my writing. God the creator is especially important in such places.*

54/55 Photo: Wall in Lindos, Island of Rhodes, Greece, 1978.

56/57 Photo: Wall in Lindos, Island of Rhodes, Greece, 1978. *With the change in these two photos I wanted to show dynamism, growth. I wanted to follow the text graphically.*

58/59 Photo: Yellow tree in field, Cariboo, British Columbia, 1977.

60/61 Photo: Dunes, Oregon, 1979.

62/63 Photo: Daisies, Burnaby, British Columbia, 1975. *This photo is a triple exposure. After each exposure I changed the position of the camera slightly, so that most of the flowers actually appear three times, side by side on the photo. Each photo was underexposed slightly, so that the three photos combined have a correct exposure.* **Text:** See also text pp. 26/27.

64/65 Photo: The bay of Lindos, Island of Rhodes, Greece, 1978.

66/67 Photo: Cariboo sky, British Columbia, 1977. *This landscape is known for its deep blue sky. To achieve an even deeper blue, I waited until just before sunset (that is why the grass is especially yellow) and then chose an angle to the sun which, when I used a polarizing filter, would shut out almost all reflected light. In other words, I did not use any color filters to intensify the blue. The landscape is real. There is nothing artificial about it.*

68/69 Photo: Oak branches, Monterey, California, 1976.

70/71 Photo: Rainbow on Isaac Lake, in the Bowron Lakes chain (see notes to pp. 52/53), British Columbia, 1978. *After the group I was with paddled strenuously to reach safety from a strong storm which had come up quickly, this beautiful rainbow appeared. One of our canoes had capsized, but no one was injured. The rainbow appeared as a sign of hope, as an indicator that there was sun above the clouds. It was reminiscent of the story told in Genesis 9, especially verse 13.*

72/73 Photo: Sunset in the dunes, Oregon, 1979. *The two people happened to wander into the frame at the right time. They are not posing.*

74/75 Photo: Nets, Vancouver, British Columbia, 1975.

76/77 Photo: Aspens in front of a dark mountainside, Cariboo, British Columbia. *To photograph this picture I had to be patient. I wanted the group of small trees in the foreground to be in the light so they would stand out against the dark background. The moment came and was gone in a few seconds, but I had caught it with my camera.*